STEVE JOBS

A Real-Life Reader Biography

Ann Gaines

Mitchell Lane Publishers, Inc.
P.O. Box 619 • Bear, Delaware 19701

Mitchell Lane PUBLISHERS

First Printing

Real-Life Reader Biographies

Selena	Robert Rodriguez	Mariah Carey	Rafael Palmeiro
Tommy Nuñez	Trent Dimas	Cristina Saralegui	Andres Galarraga
Oscar De La Hoya	Gloria Estefan	Jimmy Smits	Mary Joe Fernandez
Cesar Chavez	Chuck Norris	Sinbad	Paula Abdul
Vanessa Williams	Celine Dion	Mia Hamm	Sammy Sosa
Brandy	Michelle Kwan	Rosie O'Donnell	Shania Twain
Garth Brooks	Jeff Gordon	Mark McGwire	Salma Hayek
Sheila E.	Hollywood Hogan	Ricky Martin	Britney Spears
Arnold Schwarzenegger	Jennifer Lopez	Kobe Bryant	Derek Jeter
Steve Jobs	Sandra Bullock	Julia Roberts	Robin Williams
Jennifer Love Hewitt	Keri Russell	Sarah Michelle Gellar	Liv Tyler
Melissa Joan Hart	Drew Barrymore	Alicia Silverstone	Katie Holmes
Winona Ryder	Alyssa Milano	Freddie Prinze, Jr.	Enrique Iglesias
Christina Aguilera			

Library of Congress Cataloging-in-Publication Data
Gaines, Ann.
    Steve Jobs/Ann Gaines.
       p. cm. — (A real-life reader biography)
    ISBN 1-58415-026-2
    1. Jobs, Steven, 1955- —Juvenile literature. 2. Microcomputers—Biography—Juvenile literature. 3. Apple computer—History—Juvenile literature. [1. Jobs, Steven, 1955- 2. Computer engineers. 3. Apple Computer, Inc.] I. Title. II. Series.
QA76.2.J63 G35 2000
338.7'6100416'092—dc21
[B]
                                                  00-040534

ABOUT THE AUTHOR: Ann Gaines holds graduate degrees in American Civilization and Library and Information Science from the University of Texas at Austin. She has been a freelance writer for 18 years, specializing in nonfiction for children. She lives near Gonzales, Texas with her husband and their four children.

PHOTO CREDITS: Cover: Alan Levenson/Corbis; p. 4 Reuters/HO/Archive Photos; p. 10 Corbis/Alan Levenson; p. 17 UPI/Corbis-Bettmann; p. 20 Reuters/Lou Dematteis/Archive Photos; p. 22 Reuters/Clay McLachlan/Archive Photos; p. 26 Globe Photos; p. 28, 31 Reuters/Clay McLachlan/Archive Photos

ACKNOWLEDGMENTS: The following story has been thoroughly researched, and to the best of our knowledge, represents a true story. While every possible effort has been made to ensure accuracy, the publisher will not assume liability for damages caused by inaccuracies in the data, and makes no warranty on the accuracy of the information contained herein. This story has not been authorized by Steve Jobs or any of his representatives.

Table of Contents

Chapter 1
Born With Nothing

Steven Paul Jobs (the name rhymes with "lobs" and "gobs") made his first million dollars when he was twenty years old. He made his first billion dollars when he was forty. He was one of the most important people in two different revolutions that enrich and entertain all of us today—the development of personal computers and of animated movies.

When Steve was born, he had nothing, not even a mom and dad. His natural mother and father gave him up for adoption. He was lucky to be adopted soon afterward by some

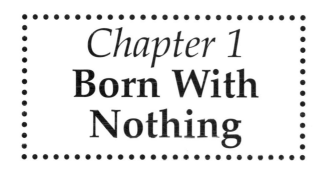

Steven Paul Jobs made his first million dollars when he was twenty years old.

wonderful people. They were great parents who respected Steve's opinions and values. They made him feel that he was important in their lives.

When he was recently asked what he wanted to pass on to his own children, Steve answered, "Just to try to be as good a father to them as my [adopted] father was to me. I think about that every day of my life." Here is the story of Steve Jobs and his quick rise to the top of the business world.

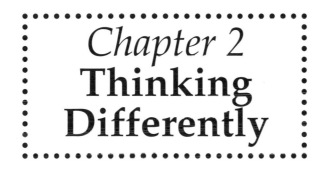

Chapter 2
Thinking Differently

Steven Paul Jobs was born on February 24, 1955. He was adopted as a very young baby by Paul and Clara Jobs. They lived on the outskirts of San Francisco, California. Like many children today, Steve grew up in a family in which both parents worked outside the home. Paul worked as a machinist for Spectra-Physics, a company that made lasers. As a kid, Steve was impressed with the way Paul could make things. He liked to watch his father fix the family car or anything else that broke around the house. It was from Paul that Steve learned to love

As a kid, Steve was impressed with the way Paul could make things.

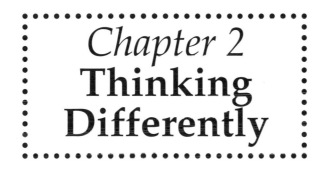

mechanics and especially electronics. His mom, Clara, worked in the offices of a local school. When Steve was five months old, the family moved to south San Francisco. Later, when Steve was five years old, the family moved a little way to the small town of Mountain View, near Palo Alto. The area later became known as the Silicon Valley, the birthplace of many giant computer companies, including Steve Jobs's future company, Apple Computer.

When Steve first went to school, he already knew much of what the other kids were just beginning to learn.

Steve grew up strong-willed and smart. His mom taught Steve to read before he went to elementary school. When he first went to school, he already knew much of what the other kids were just beginning to learn. As a result, he was bored and did not want to take part in his classmates' regular activities. One day when he was in the seventh grade, he came home from school and told his parents that he just could not stand to go anymore. To their great credit, Steve's parents took his complaint seriously. They could see that his intellectual curiosity was not being satisfied in his present school. Even though it disrupted their lives, they agreed to move to nearby Los Altos so that Steve could attend a better school. Steve's electronics teacher at Homestead High, John McCollum, recalled he was "something of a loner" and "always had a different way of looking at things."

Steve was twelve when he saw his first computer. The Hewlett-Packard Company had invited his class at school to tour the nearby company offices in Palo Alto. Steve instantly fell in love with the desktop computer that the kids were allowed to play with during the tour. He wanted one for his own. Some months later, Steve found the phone number of one of the founders of the company, William Hewlett, and called him directly. He told Hewlett who he was and asked for help in building a frequency counter—a machine that is used to measure electronic signals—for a school project. They talked for twenty minutes. Hewlett not only sent Steve the

Steve was twelve when he saw his first computer.

Steve Jobs was interested in electronics and computers at a young age.

parts for his school project, but he offered him a job at the plant during the summer of his freshman year in high school. Steve was overjoyed.

In 1969, when Steve was fourteen years old, his friend Bill Fernandez took him to meet a person who was to be very important in his life. Steven Wozniak was an electronics genius, eighteen years old at that time, and working part time at the California Department of Motor Vehicles. In his spare time "Woz" (as he was nicknamed) loved to help younger kids who were interested in building computers. Woz carefully revealed to the kids how beautiful electronic circuits were, with their resistors, bridges, gates, diodes, and transistors hooked together with wires. Steve was amazed at how much Woz knew. "Woz was the first person I met who knew more about electronics than I did," he said. The three of them would meet almost every day at Woz's house to talk about computers, or pile into Woz's car and go to the engineering library at Stanford University to read electronics books.

In 1969, computers could not be bought in the store as they are today. If you wanted a computer, you had to learn enough electronics to build one yourself. Then you would probably have to write your own software for it. Computer lovers shared their knowledge with each other openly and freely. Steve remembers those days fondly. "I was lucky to get into computers when it was a very young and idealistic industry," he said. "There

If you wanted a computer in 1969, you had to learn enough electronics to build one yourself.

Early in 1974, Steve became the fortieth employee of Atari, a computer game company that had been formed two years before.

weren't many degrees offered in computer science, so people in computers were brilliant people from mathematics, physics, music, zoology, whatever. They loved it, and no one was really in it for the money."

Steve graduated from Homestead High School in 1972 and enrolled that fall at Reed College in Portland, Oregon. He had the same kind of problems in college as he had had in grade school. He got bored with the regular classes and rules. He dropped out of school after his first semester, but remained living in the area for another year, studying the *I Ching* (an ancient Chinese book of wisdom), meditation, and vegetarianism.

Early in 1974, Steve answered an ad in the paper that said, "Have fun and make money." He was hired and became the fortieth employee of Atari Company, a computer game company that had been formed two years before to produce Pong, one of the first and most successful computer games. Steve worked on a new computer game called Breakout. Steve called Woz, and the two of them soon designed the game to use just slightly more than half of the parts Atari officials had expected. They rewarded Steve with a large bonus. Steve saved his money and went on a vacation to India with his friend, Dan Kottke. The two traveled around India in search of wise men who could teach them. But what really impressed them was the terrible poverty they saw. When they returned to the United States, Steve moved back to his hometown near Palo Alto.

Steve and Woz designed a game using slightly more than half of the parts Atari officials had expected.

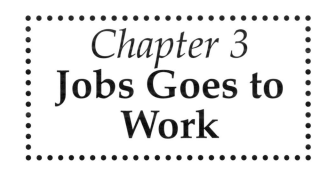

Chapter 3
Jobs Goes to Work

Steve wanted to start a business selling his computers to other people.

More and more people were becoming interested in computers and how to build them. On a rainy night in March 1975, more than thirty people, including Woz, turned out for the first meeting of the Homebrew Computer Club in Menlo Park, California, a town near Palo Alto. Steve started attending the meetings and fell in love all over again with computers. This time, Steve wanted to not only make his own computer, but also to start a business selling his computers to other people.

Steve was not alone in his vision to sell computers. Ed Roberts, an electronics technician in the Air Force, formed a company called MITS that sold electronic calculators. Early in 1974, he started selling computer kits. He made up the name "personal computer" for his computers and planned to sell them for $397. His daughter called it the Altair, after a faraway planet in the television show *Star Trek.* The computer was featured on the cover of the January 1975 issue of *Popular Electronics* magazine.

Steve talked his friend Woz into going into business with him. It was not too much of a risk for the two young men. Steve was still only twenty years old at the time, and Woz was working at Hewlett-Packard and did not have to give up his job. Woz remembered what it was like: "Basically it was like a thousand-dollar investment and we'd have to sell fifty to get our money back, because we'd build the boards for twenty dollars and sell them for forty. And boy, I remember not being sure we'd sell fifty of them at the club. But,

Steve talked his friend Woz into going into business with him.

you know, Steve thought there were surplus dealers and all that. And then finally he said, 'Even if we lose our money, at least we had a company.' And we were young back then. And when you think of it that way, you know, obviously we were going to do it. Sure, just to have a company, I'll gamble a few bucks on that. And really, we didn't take a risk—I didn't give up my job; Steve just lived at home with his parents; we didn't change our lifestyle."

In order to get the money to build their computer, Steve sold his Volkswagen microbus and Wozniak sold his calculator. They raised $1,300. They designed what would become the Apple I computer. The name for it came from a season Steve had enjoyed working in an apple orchard. Steve and Woz, along with Steve's sister and a couple of friends, built the first computers in Steve's garage. Paul Terrel, the owner of the local electronics store, bought fifty of the new machines for $500 each. They soon began selling the Apple I to other

Steve and Woz, along with Steve's sister and a couple of friends, built the first computers in Steve's garage.

computer hobbyists. In 1976, they sold 600 more. Steve, Woz, and their friends were working all the time putting the computers together. The Apple I was an advancement over the other computers that were available, like the Altair. It had a built-in video card that allowed the

computer to be connected to a television-like display. It had a special chip that told the machine how to load other programs. The Apple I was so popular that over 15,000 programs were written for it by programmers all over the world. In all, the Apple I brought in over $750,000 to the company that had started in a garage.

In 1977, the new and prosperous Apple company introduced the Apple II computer. It was designed for beginners and the public. The first personal computer with color graphics, it came with a keyboard, power supply, and monitor—everything that was needed—in one package, for $1,300. It was a success. In three years it earned $139 million.

But not every product that Apple made was an immediate success, or even a success at all. In November 1980, Apple introduced the Apple III computer. It was much more expensive than the other computers made at Apple. It was not popular and it did not always work correctly. Apple recalled 14,000 of the machines from the public and fixed what was wrong for free. The Apple III was an expensive mistake.

Chapter 4
Apple Rolls On

In December 1980, Steve began to sell parts of Apple Computer to people all over the world. To do this, the company joined the stock exchange. Each share of stock that the company sold was worth $22. They sold 46 million shares. At the end of the first day of selling stock, Apple had sold all of its shares and the value of a single share had risen to $29. In one day, Apple had become worth $1.2 billion. Steve owned 8.3 million shares of the company. In the first day Apple shares sold on the stock market, he made $239 million. He was 25 years old and fabulously wealthy. In 1982,

In December 1980, Apple Computer joined the stock exchange.

Apple Computer made Steve a fabulously wealthy man.

Apple had sales of $583 million. As of December 1982, the company's stock was selling for approximately $30 a share.

Steve now had more money than he could possibly use. He bought some expensive things, including a cool black Porsche sports car. He bought a nice home in Los Gatos, California, about twenty miles from his office in Cupertino. He did not buy much furniture for his new house. He preferred to sit on the floor in the lotus position, which is the way monks sit when they meditate. In his bedroom, Steve did not have a bed, but slept on a mattress that was placed on the floor. There was little else there. He had a lamp on the floor, an Apple II computer, and a chest of drawers for his clothes. He placed a portrait of Albert Einstein on the wall. For time off the job, he went backpacking in Yosemite National Park. Despite all of his money, Steve was still a hippie at heart.

In 1983, Apple introduced the Lisa computer. It had many new features that would soon be used by other computer makers. It had a mouse, the little handheld device used to move a pointer around the display screen and click on things on the screen. No longer would the computer operator have to use the keyboard to type hard-to-remember commands in order to make the computer work. It was a brilliant idea.

In his new house, Steve did not have a bed, but slept on a mattress that was placed on the floor.

The Lisa, like the Apple III, was not a popular success. For one thing, it cost a lot of money—$10,000. For another, it now had competition. The International Business Machine Company (IBM) had begun selling its own personal computer, the XT.

At the same time that the experts at Apple were working on the Lisa, they were also working on another, much cheaper computer called the Macintosh. It was the invention of Jeff Raskin and Burrel Smith, two of the engineers at Apple. It was named for a variety of apple, so its

Apple's new computer, The Lisa, was not a success because it was very expensive.

name was really a joke on the name of the company. It was designed to be a simple and cheap computer to be used in the home. Both the computer and the display screen came in one small box. All of the electronic circuits were placed on one circuit board. It still had the same powerful central processing unit (CPU) as the far more expensive Lisa, so it was really just as powerful and fast. It could be manufactured for less than $500.

The new Macintosh computer was introduced in January 1984. Apple had built a new factory to manufacture the computer. Steve thought that they would sell 750,000 Macs in the first year. But there were problems. There were only a few programs that would run on the new Mac. They were not the ones that a business needed. The disks that were used on the old Apple II could not be used in the new Mac. This meant that users would have to recopy all of their old work onto the new machine. The sales of the Mac were good, but not nearly as good as Steve wanted.

The new Macintosh was named for a variety of apple.

By then, other computer makers were selling far more computers than Apple. Fewer programs were being written for the Apple computers. In many ways, the Apple computers were the most advanced and most beautiful, but they were not the most popular. Soon, there were loud arguments at Apple Computer among Steve and the other leaders about whose fault it was. In 1984, he was removed from the company's board by a man he had hired named John Sculley. Jobs had hired Sculley in 1983 to help him run Apple Computer. But the two men disagreed on many things. In 1985, after one of these many arguments, Steve left and took a vacation in Europe where he rode a bicycle through France and thought about what he would do in the future. When Steve returned to the United States, he quit Apple and sold all but one share of his Apple stock for $100 million.

Chapter 5
Toy Story

While Steve was still at Apple Computer, one of his research scientists, Alan Kay, told him that the Pixar Company was for sale. Pixar was the computer division of Lucasfilm, which was owned by George Lucas, the director of the *Star Wars* movies. Pixar had been used to create some of the robots and the computer effects that Lucas wanted to use in his new movies. After Pixar had done that, Lucas wanted to sell it as a separate company. Steve wanted Apple Computer to buy Pixar, but the company executives did not think it was a good idea. But when Steve

While Steve was still at Apple Computer, he learned that the Pixar Company was for sale.

After leaving Apple Computer, Steve works with his team on ideas for his new company, NeXT.

left Apple, he bought Pixar himself for $10 million in 1986. What Steve got for his $10 million was a group of very talented animators and computer wizards. John Lasseter, who had worked on the Walt Disney movie *Tron* (which had used computer special effects), headed the talented staff. With Steve as the president of the company, Pixar quickly began to turn out successes. In 1988, Lasseter directed *Tin Toy*, a short computer-animated cartoon that won an Academy Award. In 1991, Lasseter tried to interest the Walt Disney Company, the king of cartoons, in making an hour-long cartoon for a television special. The Disney Company was so impressed with Lasseter and *Tin Toy* that they offered instead to pay for a full-length computer animation movie that would be shown in movie theaters. Steve talked to the Disney managers and they made a deal to make three movies.

The first movie they produced was *Toy Story*. It is the story of the lives of a young boy's toys when he is not around. Before the movie was finished, Steve had spent more than $50 million on Pixar. The movie first started playing in the theaters in November 1995. It was a great success. In its first week, the movie made $38 million. On November 29, 1995, Pixar sold stock in the company on the stock exchange for $22 a share. The shares quickly rose to $39 a share because so many people thought that the company was going to make money.

The first movie Pixar produced was *Toy Story*.

Steve owned 80 million shares. By Christmas 1995, Steve was worth more than $1 billion. He was only forty years old.

When Steve left Apple Computer in 1985, he also started his own company, NeXT. His goal was to build a breakthrough computer that would revolutionize research and higher

education. In October 1989, the company introduced the NeXT computer which featured many high-tech components. But it was very expensive and the company did not sell many. Within a short time, NeXT stopped hardware production. Apple Computer eventually bought NeXT for $400 million in December 1995 when they rehired Jobs as an advisor to Gilbert Amelio who had just joined Apple as CEO and chairman.

In 1997, Steve returned to Apple as its chief executive officer. Apple had been struggling in the previous decade, but Steve was able to help turn the company's fortunes around. He introduced the successful iMac computer and went on to restore consumer confidence with the introduction of the Macintosh G4 and the iBook. After losing $700 million in early 1996, Apple showed a profit in 1998. Jobs proved that his ability to run successful companies was no fluke.

Apple had been struggling in the previous decade, but Steve was able to help turn the company's fortunes around.

Chapter 6
Jobs Off the Job

While Steve was giving a talk at Stanford University in 1989, he met Laurene Powell.

While Steve was giving a talk to business students at Stanford University in 1989, he met Laurene Powell, a graduate student. The two quickly fell in love. They were married in 1991. They now live with their two children, Reed and Laurene, in a $5 million home in Palo Alto, California.

Steve had already had a child from a previous relationship. When Steve was a young man he had a baby girl with a woman he never married. The daughter's name is Lisa. She lives with them today when she is not going to college.

But Steve had even more family than he knew about. When Steve was twenty-seven years old, he found out that he had a sister two and a half years younger than he is. She is Mona Simpson, a writer. They have become close friends and talk on the telephone every couple of days. Family is very important to Steve. He has used his great wealth to bring all of the parts of his family together.

Steve is most concerned with being able to say "we've done something wonderful."

Despite his high-profile work, Steve remains a simple man with simple desires. "Being the richest man in the cemetery doesn't matter to me," he once said. "Going to bed at night saying we've done something wonderful . . . that matters to me."

Chronology

- Born Februry 24, 1955, and adopted shortly afterward by Paul and Clara Jobs.
- 1960, the Jobs family moves to Mountain View, near Palo Alto.
- 1967, sees his first computer. Calls William Hewlett of the Hewlett-Packard Company and is offered a job.
- 1969, meets Steven "Woz" Wozniak.
- 1972, graduates from high school.
- 1974, goes to work for the Atari company. Creates a computer game called Breakout.
- 1975, goes into business with Woz. They create and sell the Apple I computer.
- 1977, the company creates the Apple II.
- 1980, Apple goes public.
- 1984, Apple introduces the Macintosh. Steve resigns from Apple.
- 1986, buys the Pixar Company.
- 1991, marries Laurene Powell.
- 1995, Pixar releases the film *Toy Story*. Steve becomes a billionare at the age of forty.
- 1997, returns to Apple Computer.
- 2000, remains as interim CEO of Apple Computer as the company introduces a succession of successful computers from the iMac to the Mac G4.

Index